This Planner Belongs To:

_____

If found, please call:

_____

twenty

January

S	M	T	W	T	F	S
			1	2	3	4
5	6	7	8	9	10	11
12	13	14	15	16	17	18
19	20	21	22	23	24	25
26	27	28	29	30	31	

February

S	M	T	W	T	F	S
						1
2	3	4	5	6	7	8
9	10	11	12	13	14	15
16	17	18	19	20	21	22
23	24	25	26	27	28	29

March

S	M	T	W	T	F	S
1	2	3	4	5	6	7
8	9	10	11	12	13	14
15	16	17	18	19	20	21
22	23	24	25	26	27	28
29	30	31				

April

S	M	T	W	T	F	S
			1	2	3	4
5	6	7	8	9	10	11
12	13	14	15	16	17	18
19	20	21	22	23	24	25
26	27	28	29	30		

May

S	M	T	W	T	F	S
					1	2
3	4	5	6	7	8	9
10	11	12	13	14	15	16
17	18	19	20	21	22	23
24	25	26	27	28	29	30
31						

June

S	M	T	W	T	F	S
	1	2	3	4	5	6
7	8	9	10	11	12	13
14	15	16	17	18	19	20
21	22	23	24	25	26	27
28	29	30				

July

S	M	T	W	T	F	S
			1	2	3	4
5	6	7	8	9	10	11
12	13	14	15	16	17	18
19	20	21	22	23	24	25
26	27	28	29	30	31	

August

S	M	T	W	T	F	S
						1
2	3	4	5	6	7	8
9	10	11	12	13	14	15
16	17	18	19	20	21	22
23	24	25	26	27	28	29
30	31					

September

S	M	T	W	T	F	S
		1	2	3	4	5
6	7	8	9	10	11	12
13	14	15	16	17	18	19
20	21	22	23	24	25	26
27	28	29	30			

October

S	M	T	W	T	F	S
				1	2	3
4	5	6	7	8	9	10
11	12	13	14	15	16	17
18	19	20	21	22	23	24
25	26	27	28	29	30	31

November

S	M	T	W	T	F	S
1	2	3	4	5	6	7
8	9	10	11	12	13	14
15	16	17	18	19	20	21
22	23	24	25	26	27	28
29	30					

December

S	M	T	W	T	F	S
		1	2	3	4	5
6	7	8	9	10	11	12
13	14	15	16	17	18	19
20	21	22	23	24	25	26
27	28	29	30	31		

Password Tracker

2020

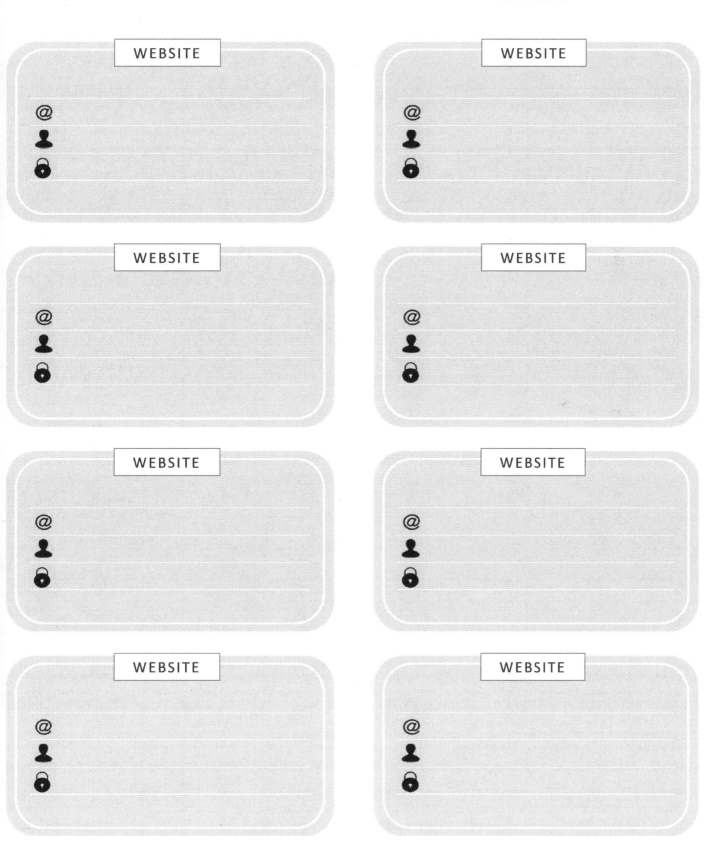

WEBSITE	WEBSITE
@	@
👤	👤
🔒	🔒

WEBSITE	WEBSITE
@	@
👤	👤
🔒	🔒

WEBSITE	WEBSITE
@	@
👤	👤
🔒	🔒

WEBSITE	WEBSITE
@	@
👤	👤
🔒	🔒

December  2019

SUNDAY	MONDAY	TUESDAY	WEDNESDAY
1	2	3	4
8	9	10	11
15	16	17	18
22	23	24	25
29	30	31	

December

2019

THURSDAY	FRIDAY	SATURDAY	NOTES
5	6	7	○
			○
			○
			○
			○
12	13	14	○
			○
			○
			○
19	20	21	○
			○
			○
			○
			○
26	27	28	○
			○
			○
			○
			○
			NOTES

January 2020

SUNDAY	MONDAY	TUESDAY	WEDNESDAY
			1
5	6	7	8
12	13	14	15
19	20	21	22
26	27	28	29

January 2020

THURSDAY	FRIDAY	SATURDAY	NOTES
2	3	4	○
			○
			○
			○
			○
9	10	11	○
			○
			○
			○
16	17	18	○
			○
			○
			○
			○
23	24	25	○
			○
			○
			○
			○
30	31		NOTES

February  2020

SUNDAY	MONDAY	TUESDAY	WEDNESDAY
2	3	4	5
9	10	11	12
16	17	18	19
23	24	25	26

February  2020

THURSDAY	FRIDAY	SATURDAY	NOTES
		1	○
			○
			○
			○
			○
6	7	8	○
			○
			○
			○
13	14	15	○
			○
			○
			○
			○
20	21	22	○
			○
			○
			○
			○
27	28	29	NOTES

March

2020

SUNDAY	MONDAY	TUESDAY	WEDNESDAY
1	2	3	4
8	9	10	11
15	16	17	18
22	23	24	25
29	30	31	

March

2020

THURSDAY	FRIDAY	SATURDAY	NOTES
5	6	7	○
			○
			○
			○
			○
12	13	14	○
			○
			○
			○
19	20	21	○
			○
			○
			○
			○
26	27	28	○
			○
			○
			○
			○
			NOTES

 # April

2020

SUNDAY	MONDAY	TUESDAY	WEDNESDAY
			1
5	6	7	8
12	13	14	15
19	20	21	22
26	27	28	29

April

2020

THURSDAY	FRIDAY	SATURDAY	NOTES
2	3	4	○
			○
			○
			○
			○
9	10	11	○
			○
			○
			○
16	17	18	○
			○
			○
			○
			○
23	24	25	○
			○
			○
			○
			○
30			NOTES

May 2020

SUNDAY	MONDAY	TUESDAY	WEDNESDAY
3	4	5	6
10	11	12	13
17	18	19	20
24	25	26	27

May 2020

THURSDAY	FRIDAY	SATURDAY	NOTES
	1	2	○
			○
			○
			○
			○
7	8	9	○
			○
			○
			○
14	15	16	○
			○
			○
			○
			○
21	22	23	○
			○
			○
			○
			○
28	29	30	NOTES
		SUNDAY 31	

June 2020

SUNDAY	MONDAY	TUESDAY	WEDNESDAY
	1	2	3
7	8	9	10
14	15	16	17
21	22	23	24
28	29	30	

June  2020

THURSDAY	FRIDAY	SATURDAY	NOTES
4	5	6	○
			○
			○
			○
			○
11	12	13	○
			○
			○
			○
18	19	20	○
			○
			○
			○
			○
25	26	27	○
			○
			○
			○
			○
			NOTES

July

SUNDAY	MONDAY	TUESDAY	WEDNESDAY
			1
5	6	7	8
12	13	14	15
19	20	21	22
26	27	28	29

July

2020

THURSDAY	FRIDAY	SATURDAY	NOTES
2	3	4	○
			○
			○
			○
			○
9	10	11	○
			○
			○
			○
16	17	18	○
			○
			○
			○
			○
23	24	25	○
			○
			○
			○
			○
30	31		NOTES

August
2020

SUNDAY	MONDAY	TUESDAY	WEDNESDAY
2	3	4	5
9	10	11	12
16	17	18	19
23 / 30	24 / 31	25	26

August

2020

THURSDAY	FRIDAY	SATURDAY	NOTES
		1	○
			○
			○
			○
			○
6	7	8	○
			○
			○
			○
			○
13	14	15	○
			○
			○
			○
			○
20	21	22	NOTES
27	28	29	

September 2020

SUNDAY	MONDAY	TUESDAY	WEDNESDAY
		1	2
6	7	8	9
13	14	15	16
20	21	22	23
27	28	29	30

September

2020

THURSDAY	FRIDAY	SATURDAY	NOTES
3	4	5	○
			○
			○
			○
			○
10	11	12	○
			○
			○
			○
17	18	19	○
			○
			○
			○
			○
24	25	26	○
			○
			○
			○
			○
			NOTES

October

2020

SUNDAY	MONDAY	TUESDAY	WEDNESDAY
4	5	6	7
11	12	13	14
18	19	20	21
25	26	27	28

October  2020

THURSDAY	FRIDAY	SATURDAY	NOTES
1	2	3	○
			○
			○
			○
			○
8	9	10	○
			○
			○
			○
15	16	17	○
			○
			○
			○
			○
22	23	24	○
			○
			○
			○
			○
29	30	31	NOTES

November 2020

SUNDAY	MONDAY	TUESDAY	WEDNESDAY
1	2	3	4
8	9	10	11
15	16	17	18
22	23	24	25
29	30		

November

2020

THURSDAY	FRIDAY	SATURDAY	NOTES
5	6	7	○
			○
			○
			○
			○
12	13	14	○
			○
			○
			○
19	20	21	○
			○
			○
			○
			○
26	27	28	○
			○
			○
			○
			○
			NOTES

December  2020

SUNDAY	MONDAY	TUESDAY	WEDNESDAY
		1	2
6	7	8	9
13	14	15	16
20	21	22	23
27	28	29	30

December  2020

THURSDAY	FRIDAY	SATURDAY	NOTES
3	4	5	○
			○
			○
			○
			○
10	11	12	○
			○
			○
			○
17	18	19	○
			○
			○
			○
			○
24	25	26	○
			○
			○
			○
			○
31			NOTES

Week Of December 29-January 4

This Week's Focus:

Notes:

Sunday	Monday	Tuesday
GOALS:	GOALS:	GOALS:

Things to Remember:

Meal Plan:

Agenda

2020

Wednesday	Thursday	Friday	Saturday
GOALS:	GOALS:	GOALS:	GOALS:

Things to Remember:

Things to Remember:

Things to Remember:

Things to Remember:

Meal Plan:

Meal Plan:

Meal Plan:

Meal Plan:

Week Of January 5-11

This Week's Focus:

Notes:

Sunday	Monday	Tuesday
GOALS:	GOALS:	GOALS:

Things to Remember: | Things to Remember: | Things to Remember:

Meal Plan: | Meal Plan: | Meal Plan:

Agenda

2020

Wednesday	Thursday	Friday	Saturday
GOALS:	GOALS:	GOALS:	GOALS:

Things to Remember:

Things to Remember:

Things to Remember:

Things to Remember:

Meal Plan:

Meal Plan:

Meal Plan:

Meal Plan:

Week Of January 12-18

This Week's Focus:

Notes:

	Sunday	Monday	Tuesday
	GOALS:	**GOALS:**	**GOALS:**

Things to Remember:

Things to Remember:

Things to Remember:

Meal Plan:

Meal Plan:

Meal Plan:

Agenda

2020

Wednesday	Thursday	Friday	Saturday
GOALS:	GOALS:	GOALS:	GOALS:

Things to Remember: Things to Remember: Things to Remember: Things to Remember:

Meal Plan: Meal Plan: Meal Plan: Meal Plan:

Week Of January 19-25

This Week's Focus:

Notes:

Sunday	Monday	Tuesday
GOALS:	GOALS:	GOALS:

Things to Remember: Things to Remember: Things to Remember:

Meal Plan: Meal Plan: Meal Plan:

Agenda

2020

Wednesday	Thursday	Friday	Saturday
GOALS:	GOALS:	GOALS:	GOALS:

Things to Remember:

Things to Remember:

Things to Remember:

Things to Remember:

Meal Plan:

Meal Plan:

Meal Plan:

Meal Plan:

Week Of January 26-February 1

This Week's Focus:

Notes:

Sunday	Monday	Tuesday
GOALS:	GOALS:	GOALS:
Things to Remember:	Things to Remember:	Things to Remember:
Meal Plan:	Meal Plan:	Meal Plan:

Agenda

2020

Wednesday	Thursday	Friday	Saturday
GOALS:	GOALS:	GOALS:	GOALS:

Things to Remember: | Things to Remember: | Things to Remember: | Things to Remember:

Meal Plan: | Meal Plan: | Meal Plan: | Meal Plan:

Week Of February 2-8

This Week's Focus:

Notes:

Sunday	Monday	Tuesday
GOALS:	GOALS:	GOALS:

Things to Remember:

Things to Remember:

Things to Remember:

Meal Plan:

Meal Plan:

Meal Plan:

Agenda

2020

Wednesday	Thursday	Friday	Saturday
GOALS:	GOALS:	GOALS:	GOALS:

Things to Remember: Things to Remember: Things to Remember: Things to Remember:

Meal Plan: Meal Plan: Meal Plan: Meal Plan:

Week Of February 9-15

Weekly

This Week's Focus:

Notes:

Sunday	Monday	Tuesday
GOALS:	GOALS:	GOALS:

Things to Remember:

Things to Remember:

Things to Remember:

Meal Plan:

Meal Plan:

Meal Plan:

Agenda

2020

Wednesday	Thursday	Friday	Saturday
GOALS:	GOALS:	GOALS:	GOALS:

Things to Remember:　Things to Remember:　Things to Remember:　Things to Remember:

Meal Plan:　Meal Plan:　Meal Plan:　Meal Plan:

Week Of February 16-22

Weekly

This Week's Focus:

Notes:

	Sunday	Monday	Tuesday
	GOALS:	GOALS:	GOALS:

Things to Remember: Things to Remember: Things to Remember:

Meal Plan: Meal Plan: Meal Plan:

Agenda

2020

Wednesday	Thursday	Friday	Saturday
GOALS:	GOALS:	GOALS:	GOALS:

Things to Remember:

Things to Remember:

Things to Remember:

Things to Remember:

Meal Plan:

Meal Plan:

Meal Plan:

Meal Plan:

Week Of February 23-29

This Week's Focus:

Notes:

	Sunday	Monday	Tuesday
GOALS:	GOALS:	GOALS:

Things to Remember:

Things to Remember:

Things to Remember:

Meal Plan:

Meal Plan:

Meal Plan:

Agenda

2020

Wednesday	Thursday	Friday	Saturday
GOALS:	GOALS:	GOALS:	GOALS:

Things to Remember: | Things to Remember: | Things to Remember: | Things to Remember:

Meal Plan: | Meal Plan: | Meal Plan: | Meal Plan:

Week Of March 1-7

This Week's Focus:

Notes:

	Sunday	Monday	Tuesday
	GOALS:	GOALS:	GOALS:

Things to Remember: Things to Remember: Things to Remember:

Meal Plan: Meal Plan: Meal Plan:

Agenda

2020

Wednesday	Thursday	Friday	Saturday
GOALS:	GOALS:	GOALS:	GOALS:

Things to Remember:

Things to Remember:

Things to Remember:

Things to Remember:

Meal Plan:

Meal Plan:

Meal Plan:

Meal Plan:

Week Of March 8-14

This Week's Focus:

Notes:

Sunday	Monday	Tuesday
GOALS:	**GOALS:**	**GOALS:**

Things to Remember: | Things to Remember: | Things to Remember:

Meal Plan: | Meal Plan: | Meal Plan:

Agenda

2020

Wednesday	Thursday	Friday	Saturday
GOALS:	GOALS:	GOALS:	GOALS:

Things to Remember: | Things to Remember: | Things to Remember: | Things to Remember:

Meal Plan: | Meal Plan: | Meal Plan: | Meal Plan:

Week Of March 15-21

This Week's Focus:

Notes:

Sunday	Monday	Tuesday
GOALS:	GOALS:	GOALS:

Things to Remember:

Things to Remember:

Things to Remember:

Meal Plan:

Meal Plan:

Meal Plan:

Agenda

2020

Wednesday	Thursday	Friday	Saturday
GOALS:	GOALS:	GOALS:	GOALS:

Things to Remember: Things to Remember: Things to Remember: Things to Remember:

Meal Plan: Meal Plan: Meal Plan: Meal Plan:

This Week's Focus:

Notes:

Sunday	Monday	Tuesday
GOALS:	GOALS:	GOALS:
Things to Remember:	Things to Remember:	Things to Remember:
Meal Plan:	Meal Plan:	Meal Plan:

Agenda

2020

Wednesday	Thursday	Friday	Saturday
GOALS:	GOALS:	GOALS:	GOALS:

Things to Remember:

Things to Remember:

Things to Remember:

Things to Remember:

Meal Plan:

Meal Plan:

Meal Plan:

Meal Plan:

Week Of March 29-April 4

This Week's Focus:

Notes:

Sunday

GOALS:

Things to Remember:

Meal Plan:

Monday

GOALS:

Things to Remember:

Meal Plan:

Tuesday

GOALS:

Things to Remember:

Meal Plan:

Agenda

Wednesday	Thursday	Friday	Saturday
GOALS:	GOALS:	GOALS:	GOALS:

Things to Remember:

Meal Plan:

Week Of April 5-11

This Week's Focus:

Notes:

	Sunday	Monday	Tuesday
	GOALS:	GOALS:	GOALS:

Things to Remember:

Things to Remember:

Things to Remember:

Meal Plan:

Meal Plan:

Meal Plan:

Agenda

2020

Wednesday	Thursday	Friday	Saturday
GOALS:	GOALS:	GOALS:	GOALS:

Things to Remember:
Things to Remember:
Things to Remember:
Things to Remember:

Meal Plan:
Meal Plan:
Meal Plan:
Meal Plan:

Week Of April 12-18

This Week's Focus:

Notes:

Sunday	Monday	Tuesday
GOALS:	GOALS:	GOALS:

Things to Remember:

Things to Remember:

Things to Remember:

Meal Plan:

Meal Plan:

Meal Plan:

Agenda

2020

Wednesday	Thursday	Friday	Saturday
GOALS:	GOALS:	GOALS:	GOALS:

Things to Remember:

Things to Remember:

Things to Remember:

Things to Remember:

Meal Plan:

Meal Plan:

Meal Plan:

Meal Plan:

Week Of April 19-25

This Week's Focus:

Notes:

Sunday	Monday	Tuesday
GOALS:	GOALS:	GOALS:

Things to Remember:

Meal Plan:

Agenda

2020

Wednesday	Thursday	Friday	Saturday
GOALS:	GOALS:	GOALS:	GOALS:

Things to Remember: | Things to Remember: | Things to Remember: | Things to Remember:

Meal Plan: | Meal Plan: | Meal Plan: | Meal Plan:

Week Of April 26-May 2

This Week's Focus:

Notes:

Sunday	Monday	Tuesday
GOALS:	GOALS:	GOALS:
Things to Remember:	Things to Remember:	Things to Remember:
Meal Plan:	Meal Plan:	Meal Plan:

Agenda

Wednesday	Thursday	Friday	Saturday
GOALS:	GOALS:	GOALS:	GOALS:

Things to Remember:

Things to Remember:

Things to Remember:

Things to Remember:

Meal Plan:

Meal Plan:

Meal Plan:

Meal Plan:

Week Of May 3-9

This Week's Focus:

Notes:

Sunday	Monday	Tuesday
GOALS:	GOALS:	GOALS:
Things to Remember:	Things to Remember:	Things to Remember:
Meal Plan:	Meal Plan:	Meal Plan:

Agenda

Wednesday	Thursday	Friday	Saturday
GOALS:	GOALS:	GOALS:	GOALS:

Things to Remember: Things to Remember: Things to Remember: Things to Remember:

Meal Plan: Meal Plan: Meal Plan: Meal Plan:

Week Of May 10-16

This Week's Focus:

Notes:

Sunday	Monday	Tuesday
GOALS:	GOALS:	GOALS:
Things to Remember:	Things to Remember:	Things to Remember:
Meal Plan:	Meal Plan:	Meal Plan:

Agenda

2020

Wednesday	Thursday	Friday	Saturday
GOALS:	GOALS:	GOALS:	GOALS:

Things to Remember: Things to Remember: Things to Remember: Things to Remember:

Meal Plan: Meal Plan: Meal Plan: Meal Plan:

This Week's Focus:

Notes:

Sunday	Monday	Tuesday
GOALS:	GOALS:	GOALS:

Things to Remember:

Things to Remember:

Things to Remember:

Meal Plan:

Meal Plan:

Meal Plan:

Agenda

Wednesday	Thursday	Friday	Saturday
GOALS:	GOALS:	GOALS:	GOALS:

Things to Remember: Things to Remember: Things to Remember: Things to Remember:

Meal Plan: Meal Plan: Meal Plan: Meal Plan:

Week Of May 24-30

This Week's Focus:

Notes:

	Sunday	Monday	Tuesday
	GOALS:	GOALS:	GOALS:

Things to Remember: Things to Remember: Things to Remember:

Meal Plan: Meal Plan: Meal Plan:

Agenda

2020

Wednesday	Thursday	Friday	Saturday
GOALS:	GOALS:	GOALS:	GOALS:

Things to Remember: Things to Remember: Things to Remember: Things to Remember:

Meal Plan: Meal Plan: Meal Plan: Meal Plan:

Week Of May 31-June 6

This Week's Focus:

Notes:

Sunday	Monday	Tuesday
GOALS:	GOALS:	GOALS:

Things to Remember:

Things to Remember:

Things to Remember:

Meal Plan:

Meal Plan:

Meal Plan:

Agenda

2020

Wednesday	Thursday	Friday	Saturday
GOALS:	GOALS:	GOALS:	GOALS:

Things to Remember: Things to Remember: Things to Remember: Things to Remember:

Meal Plan: Meal Plan: Meal Plan: Meal Plan:

Week Of June 7-13

This Week's Focus:

Notes:

Sunday	Monday	Tuesday
GOALS:	GOALS:	GOALS:

Things to Remember: Things to Remember: Things to Remember:

Meal Plan: Meal Plan: Meal Plan:

Agenda

Wednesday	Thursday	Friday	Saturday
GOALS:	GOALS:	GOALS:	GOALS:

Things to Remember: Things to Remember: Things to Remember: Things to Remember:

Meal Plan: Meal Plan: Meal Plan: Meal Plan:

Week Of June 14-20

Weekly

This Week's Focus:

Notes:

Sunday	Monday	Tuesday
GOALS:	GOALS:	GOALS:

Things to Remember:

Things to Remember:

Things to Remember:

Meal Plan:

Meal Plan:

Meal Plan:

Agenda

Wednesday	Thursday	Friday	Saturday
GOALS:	GOALS:	GOALS:	GOALS:

Things to Remember: Things to Remember: Things to Remember: Things to Remember:

Meal Plan: Meal Plan: Meal Plan: Meal Plan:

Week Of June 21-27

This Week's Focus:

Notes:

Sunday	Monday	Tuesday
GOALS:	GOALS:	GOALS:

Things to Remember:

Things to Remember:

Things to Remember:

Meal Plan:

Meal Plan:

Meal Plan:

Agenda

2020

Wednesday	Thursday	Friday	Saturday
GOALS:	GOALS:	GOALS:	GOALS:

Things to Remember: Things to Remember: Things to Remember: Things to Remember:

Meal Plan: Meal Plan: Meal Plan: Meal Plan:

Week Of June 28-July 4

This Week's Focus:

Notes:

Sunday	Monday	Tuesday
GOALS:	GOALS:	GOALS:
Things to Remember:	Things to Remember:	Things to Remember:
Meal Plan:	Meal Plan:	Meal Plan:

Agenda

2020

Wednesday	Thursday	Friday	Saturday
GOALS:	GOALS:	GOALS:	GOALS:

Things to Remember:

Things to Remember:

Things to Remember:

Things to Remember:

Meal Plan:

Meal Plan:

Meal Plan:

Meal Plan:

Week Of July 5-11

This Week's Focus:

Notes:

Sunday	Monday	Tuesday
GOALS:	GOALS:	GOALS:
....	....	....
....	....	....
....	....	....
....	....	....
....	....	....
....	....	....
....	....	....
....	....	....
Things to Remember:	Things to Remember:	Things to Remember:
Meal Plan:	Meal Plan:	Meal Plan:

Agenda

Wednesday	Thursday	Friday	Saturday
GOALS:	GOALS:	GOALS:	GOALS:

Things to Remember:

Meal Plan:

Week Of July 12-18

This Week's Focus:

Notes:

Sunday	Monday	Tuesday
GOALS:	GOALS:	GOALS:

Things to Remember: | Things to Remember: | Things to Remember:

Meal Plan: | Meal Plan: | Meal Plan:

Agenda

2020

Wednesday	Thursday	Friday	Saturday
GOALS:	GOALS:	GOALS:	GOALS:

Things to Remember:

Things to Remember:

Things to Remember:

Things to Remember:

Meal Plan:

Meal Plan:

Meal Plan:

Meal Plan:

Week Of July 19-25

Weekly

This Week's Focus:

Notes:

Sunday	Monday	Tuesday
GOALS:	GOALS:	GOALS:

Things to Remember:

Things to Remember:

Things to Remember:

Meal Plan:

Meal Plan:

Meal Plan:

Agenda

Wednesday	Thursday	Friday	Saturday
GOALS:	GOALS:	GOALS:	GOALS:

Things to Remember: | Things to Remember: | Things to Remember: | Things to Remember:

Meal Plan: | Meal Plan: | Meal Plan: | Meal Plan:

Week Of July 26-August 1

This Week's Focus:

Notes:

Sunday	Monday	Tuesday
GOALS:	GOALS:	GOALS:

Things to Remember: | Things to Remember: | Things to Remember:

Meal Plan: | Meal Plan: | Meal Plan:

Agenda

2020

Wednesday	Thursday	Friday	Saturday
GOALS:	GOALS:	GOALS:	GOALS:

Things to Remember:

Things to Remember:

Things to Remember:

Things to Remember:

Meal Plan:

Meal Plan:

Meal Plan:

Meal Plan:

Week Of August 2-8

This Week's Focus:

Notes:

	Sunday	Monday	Tuesday
	GOALS:	GOALS:	GOALS:

Things to Remember: Things to Remember: Things to Remember:

Meal Plan: Meal Plan: Meal Plan:

Agenda

2020

Wednesday	Thursday	Friday	Saturday
GOALS:	GOALS:	GOALS:	GOALS:

Things to Remember:

Meal Plan:

Things to Remember:

Meal Plan:

Things to Remember:

Meal Plan:

Things to Remember:

Meal Plan:

Week Of August 9-15

This Week's Focus:

Notes:

	Sunday	Monday	Tuesday
	GOALS:	GOALS:	GOALS:

Things to Remember: Things to Remember: Things to Remember:

Meal Plan: Meal Plan: Meal Plan:

Agenda

Wednesday	Thursday	Friday	Saturday
GOALS:	GOALS:	GOALS:	GOALS:

Things to Remember:

Things to Remember:

Things to Remember:

Things to Remember:

Meal Plan:

Meal Plan:

Meal Plan:

Meal Plan:

Week Of August 16-22

This Week's Focus:

Notes:

Sunday	Monday	Tuesday
GOALS:	GOALS:	GOALS:

Things to Remember: | Things to Remember: | Things to Remember:

Meal Plan: | Meal Plan: | Meal Plan:

Agenda

Wednesday	Thursday	Friday	Saturday
GOALS:	GOALS:	GOALS:	GOALS:

Things to Remember: | Things to Remember: | Things to Remember: | Things to Remember:

Meal Plan: | Meal Plan: | Meal Plan: | Meal Plan:

Week Of August 23-29

Weekly

This Week's Focus:

Notes:

Sunday	Monday	Tuesday
GOALS:	GOALS:	GOALS:

Things to Remember: Things to Remember: Things to Remember:

Meal Plan: Meal Plan: Meal Plan:

Agenda

Wednesday	Thursday	Friday	Saturday
GOALS:	GOALS:	GOALS:	GOALS:

Things to Remember: | Things to Remember: | Things to Remember: | Things to Remember:

Meal Plan: | Meal Plan: | Meal Plan: | Meal Plan:

Week Of August 30-September 5

This Week's Focus:

Notes:

Sunday	Monday	Tuesday
GOALS:	GOALS:	GOALS:
Things to Remember:	Things to Remember:	Things to Remember:
Meal Plan:	Meal Plan:	Meal Plan:

2020

Wednesday	Thursday	Friday	Saturday
GOALS:	**GOALS:**	**GOALS:**	**GOALS:**

Things to Remember:

Things to Remember:

Things to Remember:

Things to Remember:

Meal Plan:

Meal Plan:

Meal Plan:

Meal Plan:

Week Of September 6-12

This Week's Focus:

Notes:

Sunday	Monday	Tuesday
GOALS:	GOALS:	GOALS:

Things to Remember:

Meal Plan:

Agenda

Wednesday	Thursday	Friday	Saturday
GOALS:	GOALS:	GOALS:	GOALS:

Things to Remember:

Things to Remember:

Things to Remember:

Things to Remember:

Meal Plan:

Meal Plan:

Meal Plan:

Meal Plan:

Week Of September 13-19

Weekly

This Week's Focus:

Notes:

Sunday	Monday	Tuesday
GOALS:	GOALS:	GOALS:

Things to Remember: Things to Remember: Things to Remember:

Meal Plan: Meal Plan: Meal Plan:

Agenda

2020

Wednesday	Thursday	Friday	Saturday
GOALS:	GOALS:	GOALS:	GOALS:

Things to Remember:

Things to Remember:

Things to Remember:

Things to Remember:

Meal Plan:

Meal Plan:

Meal Plan:

Meal Plan:

Week Of September 20-26

This Week's Focus:

Notes:

Sunday
GOALS:

Things to Remember:

Meal Plan:

Monday
GOALS:

Things to Remember:

Meal Plan:

Tuesday
GOALS:

Things to Remember:

Meal Plan:

Agenda

2020

Wednesday	Thursday	Friday	Saturday
GOALS:	GOALS:	GOALS:	GOALS:

Things to Remember:

Things to Remember:

Things to Remember:

Things to Remember:

Meal Plan:

Meal Plan:

Meal Plan:

Meal Plan:

Week Of September 27-October 3

This Week's Focus:

Notes:

Sunday	Monday	Tuesday
GOALS:	GOALS:	GOALS:
Things to Remember:	Things to Remember:	Things to Remember:
Meal Plan:	Meal Plan:	Meal Plan:

Agenda

2020

Wednesday	Thursday	Friday	Saturday
GOALS:	GOALS:	GOALS:	GOALS:

Things to Remember: | Things to Remember: | Things to Remember: | Things to Remember:

Meal Plan: | Meal Plan: | Meal Plan: | Meal Plan:

Week Of October 4-10

This Week's Focus:

Notes:

Sunday	Monday	Tuesday
GOALS:	GOALS:	GOALS:

Things to Remember:

Meal Plan:

Things to Remember:

Meal Plan:

Things to Remember:

Meal Plan:

Agenda

Wednesday	Thursday	Friday	Saturday
GOALS:	GOALS:	GOALS:	GOALS:

Things to Remember: | Things to Remember: | Things to Remember: | Things to Remember:

Meal Plan: | Meal Plan: | Meal Plan: | Meal Plan:

Week Of October 11-17

Weekly

This Week's Focus:

Notes:

Sunday	Monday	Tuesday
GOALS:	GOALS:	GOALS:

Things to Remember: Things to Remember: Things to Remember:

Meal Plan: Meal Plan: Meal Plan:

Agenda

Wednesday	Thursday	Friday	Saturday
GOALS:	GOALS:	GOALS:	GOALS:

Things to Remember: Things to Remember: Things to Remember: Things to Remember:

Meal Plan: Meal Plan: Meal Plan: Meal Plan:

Week Of October 18-24

This Week's Focus:

Notes:

Sunday

GOALS:

Things to Remember:

Meal Plan:

Monday

GOALS:

Things to Remember:

Meal Plan:

Tuesday

GOALS:

Things to Remember:

Meal Plan:

Agenda

2020

Wednesday	Thursday	Friday	Saturday
GOALS:	GOALS:	GOALS:	GOALS:

Things to Remember: | Things to Remember: | Things to Remember: | Things to Remember:

Meal Plan: | Meal Plan: | Meal Plan: | Meal Plan:

Week Of October 25-31

Weekly

This Week's Focus:

Notes:

Sunday	Monday	Tuesday
GOALS:	GOALS:	GOALS:
Things to Remember:	Things to Remember:	Things to Remember:
Meal Plan:	Meal Plan:	Meal Plan:

Agenda

2020

Wednesday	Thursday	Friday	Saturday
GOALS:	GOALS:	GOALS:	GOALS:

Things to Remember: | Things to Remember: | Things to Remember: | Things to Remember:

Meal Plan: | Meal Plan: | Meal Plan: | Meal Plan:

Week Of November 1-7

This Week's Focus:

Notes:

Sunday	Monday	Tuesday
GOALS:	GOALS:	GOALS:

Things to Remember:

Things to Remember:

Things to Remember:

Meal Plan:

Meal Plan:

Meal Plan:

Agenda

2020

Wednesday	Thursday	Friday	Saturday
GOALS:	GOALS:	GOALS:	GOALS:

Things to Remember: | Things to Remember: | Things to Remember: | Things to Remember:

Meal Plan: | Meal Plan: | Meal Plan: | Meal Plan:

Week Of November 8-14

This Week's Focus:

Notes:

	Sunday	Monday	Tuesday
	GOALS:	GOALS:	GOALS:

Things to Remember:

Things to Remember:

Things to Remember:

Meal Plan:

Meal Plan:

Meal Plan:

Agenda

Wednesday	Thursday	Friday	Saturday
GOALS:	GOALS:	GOALS:	GOALS:

Things to Remember:

Things to Remember:

Things to Remember:

Things to Remember:

Meal Plan:

Meal Plan:

Meal Plan:

Meal Plan:

Week Of November 15-21

Weekly

This Week's Focus:

Notes:

Sunday	Monday	Tuesday
GOALS:	GOALS:	GOALS:

Things to Remember:

Things to Remember:

Things to Remember:

Meal Plan:

Meal Plan:

Meal Plan:

Agenda

2020

Wednesday	Thursday	Friday	Saturday
GOALS:	GOALS:	GOALS:	GOALS:

Things to Remember:

Things to Remember:

Things to Remember:

Things to Remember:

Meal Plan:

Meal Plan:

Meal Plan:

Meal Plan:

Week Of November 22-28

This Week's Focus:

Notes:

Sunday	Monday	Tuesday
GOALS:	GOALS:	GOALS:
Things to Remember:	Things to Remember:	Things to Remember:
Meal Plan:	Meal Plan:	Meal Plan:

Agenda

2020

Wednesday	Thursday	Friday	Saturday
GOALS:	GOALS:	GOALS:	GOALS:

Things to Remember: Things to Remember: Things to Remember: Things to Remember:

Meal Plan: Meal Plan: Meal Plan: Meal Plan:

Week Of November 29-December 5

This Week's Focus:

Notes:

Sunday	Monday	Tuesday
GOALS:	GOALS:	GOALS:

Things to Remember:

Things to Remember:

Things to Remember:

Meal Plan:

Meal Plan:

Meal Plan:

Agenda

2020

Wednesday	Thursday	Friday	Saturday
GOALS:	GOALS:	GOALS:	GOALS:

Things to Remember: | Things to Remember: | Things to Remember: | Things to Remember:

Meal Plan: | Meal Plan: | Meal Plan: | Meal Plan:

Week Of December 6-12

This Week's Focus:

Notes:

Sunday	Monday	Tuesday
GOALS:	GOALS:	GOALS:

Things to Remember: Things to Remember: Things to Remember:

Meal Plan: Meal Plan: Meal Plan:

Agenda

2020

Wednesday	Thursday	Friday	Saturday
GOALS:	GOALS:	GOALS:	GOALS:

Things to Remember:

Things to Remember:

Things to Remember:

Things to Remember:

Meal Plan:

Meal Plan:

Meal Plan:

Meal Plan:

Week Of December 13-19

Weekly

This Week's Focus:

Notes:

Sunday	Monday	Tuesday
GOALS:	GOALS:	GOALS:

Things to Remember: Things to Remember: Things to Remember:

Meal Plan: Meal Plan: Meal Plan:

Agenda

2020

Wednesday	Thursday	Friday	Saturday
GOALS:	GOALS:	GOALS:	GOALS:

Things to Remember: | Things to Remember: | Things to Remember: | Things to Remember:

Meal Plan: | Meal Plan: | Meal Plan: | Meal Plan:

Week Of December 20-26

This Week's Focus:

Notes:

	Sunday	Monday	Tuesday
	GOALS:	GOALS:	GOALS:

Things to Remember:

Things to Remember:

Things to Remember:

Meal Plan:

Meal Plan:

Meal Plan:

Agenda

Wednesday	Thursday	Friday	Saturday
GOALS:	GOALS:	GOALS:	GOALS:

Things to Remember: Things to Remember: Things to Remember: Things to Remember:

Meal Plan: Meal Plan: Meal Plan: Meal Plan:

Week Of December 27-January 2

Weekly

This Week's Focus:

Notes:

Sunday	Monday	Tuesday
GOALS:	GOALS:	GOALS:

Things to Remember:

Things to Remember:

Things to Remember:

Meal Plan:

Meal Plan:

Meal Plan:

Agenda

2020

Wednesday	Thursday	Friday	Saturday
GOALS:	GOALS:	GOALS:	GOALS:

Things to Remember:

Things to Remember:

Things to Remember:

Things to Remember:

Meal Plan:

Meal Plan:

Meal Plan:

Meal Plan:

Year in Pixels

	J	F	M	A	M	J	J	A	S	O	N	D
1.												
2.												
3.												
4.												
5.												
6.												
7.												
8.												
9.												
10.												
11.												
12.												
13.												
14.												
15.												
16.												
17.												
18.												
19.												
20.												
21.												
22.												
23.												
24.												
25.												
26.												
27.												
28.												
29.												
30.												
31.												

Color Codes

Notes

Made in the USA
Monee, IL
07 October 2020

44257537R00077